MY BOOK OF
Stories

write your own Shakespearean tales

First published in 2016 by
The British Library
96 Euston Road
London NW1 2DB

ISBN 978 0 7123 5634 3

British Library Cataloguing in Publication Data
A catalogue record for this book is available from the British Library

Designed by Perfect Bound Ltd
Picture research by Sally Nicholls

Printed in Hong Kong by Great Wall Printing Co. Ltd

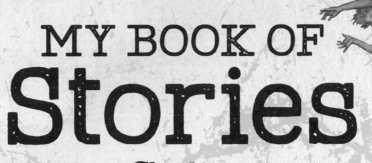

MY BOOK OF
Stories

write your own Shakespearean tales

Thanks to Jacqui O'Hanlon, Director of
Education, Royal Shakespeare Company, for
her help with the Shakespearean words

For Neil, who took on more than
his fair share of bathtimes

Contents

Introduction: My Book of Stories

My Book of Stories is full of inspirational ways to start your own stories. Snippets of text collected from some of the best stories ever written such as *Cinderella*, *Romeo and Juliet*, and *The Wizard of Oz*, have been paired with story suggestions about how to write what happens next. Top tips on how to write a story, and lists of inspirational words used by expert authors such as Shakespeare, Lewis Carroll and J.K. Rowling, will help you along your way.

If you've ever read a book, but wondered what would happen if the hero decided to go left, not right, or wanted to give a minor character more to do, then this is the series for you.

On your story-writing journey you'll find fun puzzles to do, silly lists and tidbits of information about authors and their books.

So you want to sit down
and write some stories?

What do you need?

A pen, some paper,
and then what?

You need to decide what
to write about.
Where do you start?

Top 5 inspirational story starters

1. *Real-life stories*
2. *Myths and fairy tales*
3. *The world around you*
4. *A book that you've read*
5. *Your own interests, such as sport, music, films*

Ready to get scribbling??

Introduction:
Write your own Shakespearean tales

I'm sure you've heard of William Shakespeare. He wrote plays and poems over 400 years ago. He was born in 1564 in Stratford-upon-Avon, in England. Queen Elizabeth I was on the throne at the time. He wrote around 38 plays, including *Macbeth*, *A Midsummer Night's Dream* and *Romeo and Juliet*. He also wrote about 154 sonnets, which are short poems, and a couple of longer poems too.

Shakespeare was an actor and playwright (someone who writes plays) for a company of actors called the Lord Chamberlain's Men. In 1598 they built a new theatre called the Globe on the south bank of the Thames in London. In Shakespeare's time people didn't sit and watch plays quietly. Many of the audience would be standing up in front of the stage and they would boo and jeer the actors as well as laughing at jokes and clapping their approval.

Shakespeare often borrowed plot lines for his plays and was inspired by existing stories. He wrote about real historical events and characters, including English royalty and Greek and Roman rulers. Perhaps Shakespeare's words can inspire you to write your own Shakespearean tales?

Shakespeare wrote stories about magical creatures, witches and ghosts. He wrote love stories, funny stories and stories about kings, queens, princes and princesses. In the pages that follow you'll have the chance to write your own stories, poems, diary entries and comic strips, all inspired by Shakespeare's characters, language and plots.

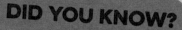

DID YOU KNOW?

A replica of Shakespeare's original Globe Theatre was built, just a short distance away from where it originally stood. It opened in 1997, and you can still go and see plays performed there today, just as people would have watched Shakespeare acting on stage.

DID YOU KNOW?

In Shakespeare's time women's parts were played by boys as there were no women actors.

Here are all of the Shakespeare plays quoted in My Book of Stories and a brief description of what happens in them.

Antony and Cleopatra

Roman leader, Antony, has an affair with Egypt's glamorous queen, Cleopatra. His actions lead to a bitter war and the tragic death of the main characters.

As You Like It

A comedy set in the Forest of Arden where Rosalind tries to find her exiled father, and also woos her true love, Orlando, while in disguise as a boy.

The Comedy of Errors

Two pairs of identical twins cause havoc and confusion in the town of Ephesus.

Cymbeline

The fairy-tale characters include a wicked stepmother and long-lost brothers, but it is Imogen's love for Posthumus that is at the heart of the play.

Hamlet

Prince of Denmark, Hamlet, wants to take revenge on his Uncle Claudius, whom he knows killed his father.

Henry IV, Part I

Prince Hal, son of Henry IV, is divided between youthful rebellion and duty to king and country. Falstaff, Hal's drinking buddy, is one of Shakespeare's best comic characters.

Henry V

King Henry V leads his troops to victory against the French in the Battle of Agincourt.

Love's Labour's Lost

The King of Navarre and three nobleman swear off love for three years in order to devote themselves to study just as four attractive women arrive to stay at the castle.

Macbeth

Following the witches' prophesy Macbeth and Lady Macbeth murder the king, but their ambition leads to their downfall.

The Merry Wives of Windsor

A farcical comedy in which Falstaff (the same Falstaff who was friends with Prince Hal in *Henry IV, Part I*) tries to woo two married women for their money.

A Midsummer Night's Dream

Four unhappy lovers enter a magical forest where a fairy king quarrels with a fairy queen and a magic flower makes people fall in love.

Much Ado About Nothing

Beatrice and Benedick hide their true feelings behind a series of witty remarks and insults, but by the end of the play their love for each other is revealed.

Richard II

Richard II is a weak king who doesn't manage his money well and doesn't know how to rule the country. As a result he loses the crown.

Romeo and Juliet

Romeo and Juliet fall in love and marry, despite coming from warring families. Their tragic story ends with their deaths.

The Tempest

Miranda lives on an island with her magician father, Prospero. He conjures up a storm to shipwreck those who banished him and his daughter from their home.

Twelfth Night

Viola is shipwrecked in Illyria, then disguises herself as a boy before going to work for Duke Orsino.

The Winter's Tale

A jealous husband, a long-lost daughter brought up by shepherds, a wife who feigns death and a happy ending!

There's magic in the web of it

(Othello)

We would all love the chance to do something magical, whether it's teleporting to avoid the walk to school, turning a frog into a prince, or being able to fly.

Stories of wizards and magicians, fairies and witches didn't start with Shakespeare, and certainly didn't end with him. From the fairy tales of Hans Christian Andersen to **The Lion, the Witch and the Wardrobe**, to **Harry Potter and the Philosopher's Stone** we all love a good story with a magical twist. In Shakespeare's plays we can find witches, fairies and sorcerers. We find ethereal ghosts, spirits and sprites. Sometimes magic in Shakespeare's stories is used for good, but mostly it is used for making mischief, such as Puck's in **A Midsummer Night's Dream**, or for evil, just think of those haggard witches in **Macbeth**. Enjoy reading the words of these magical creatures and creating your own spellbinding stories.

List your top 5 magical books

1. ....
2. ....
3. ....
4. ....
5. ....

Top 5 fictional witches

The Grand High Witch
(Roald Dahl's The Witches)

The Wicked Witch of the West
(L. Frank Baum's The Wonderful Wizard of Oz)

Hermione Granger
(J.K. Rowling's Harry Potter series)

The Three Witches
(Shakespeare's Macbeth)

Mildred Hubble
(Jill Murphy's The Worst Witch)

A Fairy song from
A Midsummer Night's Dream

You spotted snakes with double tongue,
Thorny hedgehogs, be not seen;
Newts and blindworms, do no wrong;
Come not near our Fairy Queen.
Weaving spiders, come not here;
Hence, you long-legged spinners, hence;
Beetles black, approach not near;
Worm nor snail do no offence.
Philomel with melody,
Sing in our sweet lullaby;
Lulla, lulla, lullaby; lulla, lulla, lullaby.
Never harm,
Nor spell nor charm
Come our lovely lady nigh.
So good night, with lullaby.

(Act II, Scene 2 – *The Fairies sing*)

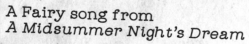

DID YOU KNOW?

Titania's fairies are called Peaseblossom,
Moth, Cobweb and Mustardseed.
What are your fairies called?

Write your own fairy song

Try using some of these Shakespearean fairy words in your song.

pearl
cowslip
rubies
queen
moon
favours
dewdrops
freckles

Imagine you are a sprite like Puck

Edited excerpt from *A Midsummer Night's Dream*, Act II, Scene 1

Fairy: Either I mistake your shape and making quite,
Or else you are that shrewd and knavish sprite...

Puck: Thou speak'st aright;
I am that merry wanderer of the night.
I jest to Oberon and make him smile
When I a fat and bean-fed horse beguile,
Neighing in likeness of a filly foal:
And sometime lurk I in a gossip's bowl,
In very likeness of a roasted crab,
And when she drinks, against her lips I bob
And on her wither'd dewlap pour the ale.
The wisest aunt, telling the saddest tale,
Sometime for three-foot stool mistaketh me;
Then slip I from her bum, down topples she...

Puck is a sprite who changes his form to play tricks on people to entertain his master, Oberon, King of the Fairies. In the quote above he describes becoming a stool, a female horse and even a roasted crab. The crab makes the drinker of the soup spill the liquid, the filly teases the male horse and the stool falls away, making the aunt fall on the floor.

Write a story of a trick that you play on someone.

What happens next?

What instructions does Prospero give Ariel, and what happens when he carries them out?

Edited excerpt from *The Tempest*, Act I, Scene 2

Prospero: Come away, servant, come; I am ready now.
Approach, my Ariel. Come.

Enter Ariel. ←............................... stage direction

Ariel: All hail, great master, grave sir, hail! I come
To answer thy best pleasure; be't to fly,
To swim, to dive into the fire, to ride
On the curl'd clouds. To thy strong bidding,
task Ariel . . .

. . . What shall I do? Say what? What shall I do?

Prospero:

_____

_____

_____

_____

_____

_____

_____

_____

_____

_____

Ideas for Prospero's instructions from The Tempest

- Be invisible and spy on people
- Become flames of fire
- Create a storm at sea
- Create magical music anywhere
- Make people fall asleep

Write a story of a magical statue

Draw a picture of your statue here

Edited excerpt from *The Winter's Tale*, Act V, Scene 3

Paulina: Music! Awake her! Strike! .... *stage direction*

Music. ←..........

'Tis time; descend; be stone no more; approach;
Strike all that look upon with marvel. Come;
I'll fill your grave up. Stir; nay, come away;
Bequeath to death your numbness; for from him
Dear life redeems you. You perceive she stirs.

Hermione comes down. ←.......... *stage direction*

Leontes: O, she's warm!

It's complicated!

Hermione pretended to be dead because her baby daughter was taken away from her, her young son had died and her husband believed that she had been having an affair. In fact she hid away for 16 years, with the help of Paulina, only agreeing to return when her daughter was found. When all of the characters are reconciled at the end of the play Paulina turns Hermione into a magical statue so that she may surprise her husband.

Excerpt from the witches' spell from
Macbeth, **Act IV, Scene 1**

All: Double, double toil and trouble;
Fire burn, and cauldron bubble.

Second Witch: Fillet of a fenny snake,
In the cauldron boil and bake;
Eye of newt, and toe of frog,
Wool of bat, and tongue of dog,
Adder's fork, and blind-worm's sting,
Lizard's leg, and howlet's wing –
For a charm of pow'rful trouble,
Like a hell-broth boil and bubble.

All: Double, double toil and trouble;
Fire burn, and cauldron bubble.

Write a wicked spell

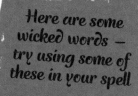

Here are some
wicked words —
try using some of
these in your spell

poison
toad
moon
gruel
foul
black
spirit
prick
blood
hag
flame
curse
fog
venom
charm
dragon

Can you be as insulting as the Bard?

"Thou art like a toad; ugly and venomous."

"Thou art a flesh-monger, a fool and a coward."

"You scullion! You rampallian! You fustilarian!"

"Thou clay-brained guts, thou knotty-pated fool, thou whoreson obscene greasy tallow-catch!"

Create your own Shakespearean insults using the words below. Take a word from column A, then B and then C, put thou in front of it, and you have the perfect villainous insult.

COLUMN A	COLUMN B	COLUMN C
bawdy	bat-fowling	barnacle
cockered	boil-brained	bum-bailey
goatish	dizzy-eyed	clack-dish
loggerheaded	flap-mouthed	flax-wench
puking	idle-headed	horn-beast
mangled	pox-marked	malt-worm
rank	onion-eyed	measle
roguish	rude-growing	pigeon-egg
weedy	sheep-biting	pignut
spleeny	toad-spotted	wagtail

We've started you off . . .

25

This is how Trinculo describes Caliban when he first sees him:

What have we here? A man or a fish? Dead or alive? A fish, he smells like a fish; a very ancient and fish-like smell; a kind of, not-of-the-newest poor-John...Legg'd like a man; and his fins like arms...this is no fish, but an islander, that hath lately suffer'd by a thunderbolt.

Questions to think about before you write
- What is his superpower?
- Does he have a superhero outfit?
- What or who does he save?
- What or who is the villain?

IN *THE TEMPEST* CALIBAN,
A WITCH'S SON, IS PROSPERO'S
SLAVE, BUT IN THIS COMIC STRIP
HE CAN BE A SUPERHERO.

Draw a picture of
your superhero here

ARRRGGH!

SUDDENLY...

NOOOOo!

Hold the front page!!

Edited excerpt from *Hamlet*, Act I, Scene 4

Enter Ghost.

Horatio: Look, my lord, it comes!

Hamlet: Angels and ministers of grace defend us!
Be thou a spirit of health, or goblin damn'd,
Bring with thee airs from heaven,
or blasts from hell,
Be thy intents wicked, or charitable,
Thou com'st in such a questionable shape
That I will speak to thee. I'll call thee Hamlet,
King, father, royal Dane. O, answer me!

Ghost beckons Hamlet.

Imagine you are a newspaper editor and one of your best journalists calls in the following story:

"Prince Hamlet saw the ghost of his father, the late King of Denmark, on the battlements of the castle tonight. The ghost told him that he had been murdered by his brother Claudius. As you already know, Claudius married Hamlet's mother, Queen Gertrude, only one month after the King's death, so now **he** is the King of Denmark. The ghost has apparently told Hamlet to seek revenge on Claudius."

Write and design a front page that will grab the reader's attention.

The Danish Daily

Write your own ghostly scene

Macbeth is horrified when the ghost of Banquo, who he has had murdered, sits in his seat at a banquet. Imagine a scene at a party where everyone is seated, but one of those seats is taken up by a ghost. Write the scene as the host enters the room and sees the ghost for the first time.

Excerpt from *Macbeth*, Act III, Scene 4

Macbeth: Avaunt, and quit my sight. Let the earth hide thee.
Thy bones are marrowless, thy blood is cold;
Thou hast no speculation in those eyes
Which thou dost glare with!

Questions to think about before you write

- Is it a friendly ghost or a wicked one?
- What does it look like?
- Does it have a name?
- What kind of party is it?
- Does the ghost cause mischief?

Write your own mythical creature story

These pages are for you to fill with your own story of magical creatures. Will you write about a sprite or a ghost, or perhaps your story will be about something coming to life? Maybe you'll choose to write a story of witches and wizards.

TOP TIP
Think about your story mountain before you write.

3 The Problem - what goes wrong?

2 The Build-up - what are your characters doing?

4 The Resolution - how the problem is fixed

1 The Beginning - introduce your characters and the setting

5 The Ending - is it a happy ending? Have the characters learnt a lesson?

Write your story's title here

_____

_____
_____
_____
_____
_____
_____
_____
_____
_____
_____
_____
_____
_____
_____
_____
_____

Turn the page for more room to write

Can you find these magical Shakespearean characters in this wordsearch?

ARIEL
CALIBAN
COBWEB
FAIRY
GHOST
OBERON
PROSPERO
PUCK
SPRITE
WITCH

```
O R E P S O R P C E V C V Y S
N U C W Z D H A Z U O O M D F
R O G T A P L P V Y W B B R R
U F R W Q I S D Z P Y W A M I
T W K E B S P R I T E E R N D
Y E I A B L S G E S G B I I M
Q K N T P O H Y R I A F E U P
B C G R C O M B W Q R Q L Z S
E D R O S H J O P L U L X S Q
B S N T X P H Q J U E X T W M
S A L O Y Z P T M F I J T G A
L P Q D H R U W M L X H Z X W
P O R C N H C N W O N A B H S
S M Q A U G K P Q S M C V I H
B U Z Z A F I M K P S B U K M
```

The course of true love . . .

Stories of love are timeless, and it turns out that Shakespeare had an awful lot to say on the topic – forbidden love, jealous love, love-sickness, unrequited love . . . There are characters who are unlucky in love, others who are lucky. A few live happily ever after while others are doomed to a 'death-mark'd love' (*Romeo and Juliet*).

As Shakespeare says, 'The course of true love never did run smooth' and in the following pages you'll see many examples of this. From a fairy queen falling in love with a mortal with a donkey's head to friends who cannot admit their love for one another, and the ultimate forbidden love as portrayed by Romeo and Juliet.

Poetry is often used as a way to express love, and Shakespeare is no exception to this. His characters use poetry to declare their love, and Shakespeare's own sonnets are full of passion and romantic expressions.

Arm yourself with words of love and enjoy creating your own stories. Will yours have a happy ending?

Top 5 Shakespearean love quotations

I know no ways to mince it in love,
but directly to say "I love you" (Henry V)

Who ever loved that loved not at first sight?
(As You Like It)

I love you with so much of my heart that none is
left to protest (Much Ado About Nothing)

But love is blind and lovers cannot see . . .
(The Merchant of Venice)

It is my lady, O, it is my love!
(Romeo and Juliet)

Top 3 Shakespearean places to declare your love

From street level up to a balcony

At a masked ball

By pinning poetry up in a forest

TOP 3 MODERN-DAY WAYS TO DECLARE YOUR LOVE

A public message at a live sports event

At a fancy-dress party

A post on social media

Write a letter

ROMEO AND JULIET ARE "A PAIR OF STAR-CROSS'D LOVERS". LIVING IN VERONA, ITALY. ROMEO IS FROM THE MONTAGUE FAMILY. JULIET FROM THE CAPULETS. UNFORTUNATELY FOR THE LOVERS THEIR TWO FAMILIES ARE SWORN ENEMIES.

Imagine you are either Romeo or Juliet. Write a letter to your best friend who lives in a different city telling them about your new-found love, and the problem that they come from the wrong family.

Romeo: Is she a Capulet?
O dear account! my life is my foe's debt.

Juliet: Come hither, Nurse, what is yond gentleman?
Nurse: His name is Romeo, and a Montague,
The only son of your great enemy.
Juliet: My only love sprung from my only hate,
Too early seen, unknown, and known too late,
Prodigious birth of love it is to me,
That I must love a loathed enemy...

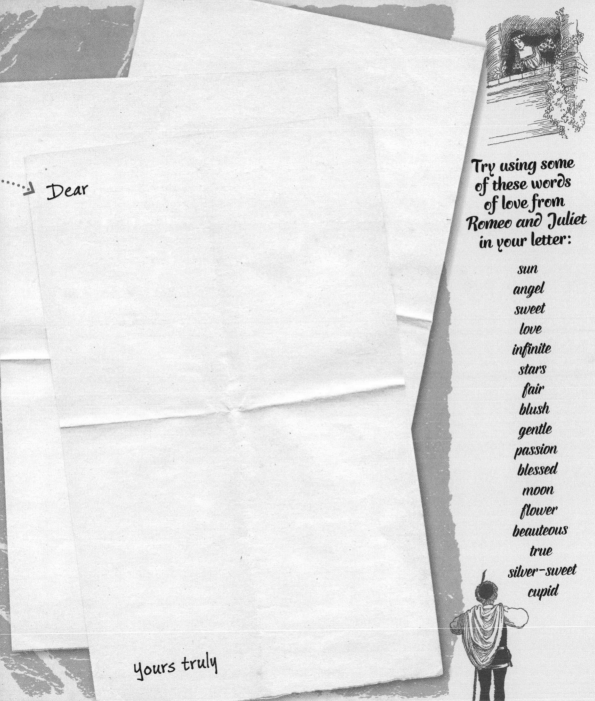

..... Dear

Yours truly

Try using some
of these words
of love from
Romeo and Juliet
in your letter:

sun
angel
sweet
love
infinite
stars
fair
blush
gentle
passion
blessed
moon
flower
beauteous
true
silver-sweet
cupid

Write a love poem

Orlando is a teenager in love with the beautiful Rosalind. Instead of writing graffiti on the back of bathroom doors he writes cheesy love poems about Rosalind and pins them on trees in the forest.

One of Orlando's poems from *As You Like It*, Act III, Scene 2

From the east to western Inde,
No jewel is like Rosalind.
Her worth, being mounted on the wind,
Through all the world bears Rosalind.
All the pictures fairest lin'd
Are but black to Rosalind.
Let no face be kept in mind
But the fair of Rosalind.

TOP TIP

Read the poem aloud. Did you notice it's written in rhyming couplets? A rhyming couplet is two lines within a poem, where the last word in each line rhymes.

Try writing your love poem in rhyming couplets

Here are some
rhymes from some
of Orlando's other
love poems

love : dove
heart : part
sprite : write
no : show
majesty : modesty
friend : end

Write a story about giving something up

RULES OF STUDY

Live and study here three years
Not to see a woman in that term
One day in a week to touch no food
Sleep but three hours in the night

Quotations from Love's Labour's Lost,
Act I, Scene 1

King Ferdinand of Navarre, a kingdom near Spain, swears an oath with his three courtiers, Longaville, Dumaine and Berowne, to devote themselves to studying for three years. In order to focus themselves completely on their studies the King makes them all agree to avoid women.

Questions to think about before you write

■ What is the goal your character is going for? It could be a big event such as performing in a play, taking an important exam or test, or competing in a sporting event.

■ What will your character give up or avoid in order to keep focused? Chocolate, television, their best friend?

Sonnets

Shakespeare is famous for writing a type of rhyming poem called a sonnet – and lots of them . . . 154 in total!

A sonnet is written to a very strict format.
A sonnet has 14 lines.
Each line has 10 syllables.
The rhymes must follow this pattern:

Lines 1 and 3	Rhyme A
Lines 2 and 4	Rhyme B
Lines 5 and 7	Rhyme C
Lines 6 and 8	Rhyme D
Lines 9 and 11	Rhyme E
Lines 10 and 12	Rhyme F
Lines 13 and 14	Rhyme G

How many syllables can you count in these words?

Diplodocus

Terrific

Supercalifragilisticexpialidocious

WHAT IS A SYLLABLE?

The word dog has
1 syllable (dog)
The word daisy has
2 syllables (dai/sy)
The word elephant has
3 syllables (El/e/phant)

TOP TIP

Say the words out loud and count the syllables on your fingers as you do.

44

Sonnet 18 is one of Shakespeare's most famous sonnets

Shall I compare thee to a summer's day?
Thou art more lovely and more temperate.
Rough winds do shake the darling buds of May,
And summer's lease hath all too short a date.
Sometime too hot the eye of heaven shines,
And often is his gold complexion dimmed;
And every fair from fair sometime declines,
By chance, or nature's changing course, untrimmed;
But thy eternal summer shall not fade,
Nor lose possession of that fair thou owest,
Nor shall death brag thou wanderest in his shade,
When in eternal lines to time thou growest.
   So long as men can breathe or eyes can see,
   So long lives this, and this gives life to thee.

Can you see how the rhymes follow the rhyming pattern? Rhyme A is "day" and "May"; Rhyme B is "temperate" and "date" and so on. The exception is the last two lines which must rhyme with each other, so Rhyme G is "see" and "thee".

This poem starts by comparing his beloved to a summer's day, but then goes on to explain that a summer's day isn't perfect. A day in May can be windy, the sun can be obscured by cloud and, most crucially, a summer's day comes to an end. In order to allow his beloved to live past the end of summer, and until the end of time, he has written this sonnet about her which will keep her alive as long as people are around to read it.

Write a sonnet

Shakespeare chose to compare his beloved to a summer's day, but what about choosing a different season? You could start your sonnet with one of these first lines instead:

Shall I compare thee to a bright spring day?
Shall I compare thee to an autumn day?
Shall I compare thee to a winter's day?

Shakespeare rhymes day with May. What else could you rhyme day with?

What happens next?

Quoted from *A Midsummer Night's Dream*, Act II, Scene 2

Oberon: *(as he drops the magic plant juice on to Titania's eyes while she sleeps)*

What thou seest when thou dost wake,
Do it for thy true-love take,
Love and languish for his sake:
Be it ounce, or cat, or bear,
Pard, or boar with bristled hair,
In thy eye that shall appear
When thou wakest, it is thy dear;
Wake when some vile thing is near.

Oberon, the king of the fairies, is cross with his queen, Titania, so he instructs his fairy servant, Puck, to bring him a magic plant, the juice of which will, when dropped on to her eyes, make her fall in love with the first thing she sees when she wakes up. Puck adds a little extra mischief to this – he casts a spell on another character in the play, called Bottom, giving him a donkey's head. When Titania wakes, Bottom is the first thing she sees.

Quoted from *A Midsummer Night's Dream*, Act III, Scene 1

Titania: *(Awaking)* What angel wakes me from my flowery bed?

Questions to think about before you write

- Does Bottom know he has a donkey's head?
- Does Bottom also fall in love with Titania?
- Does the magic fade at some point in your story?
- Do they live happily ever after?

Write a declaration of love

Benedick and Beatrice argue throughout the play, *Much Ado About Nothing*. Their friends all think they are falling in love, but they insist they are not. By the end of the play their friends trick them into revealing their love for each other, and they plan to marry.

Edited excerpt from *Much Ado About Nothing*, Act V, Scene 4

Benedick: Do not you love me?

Beatrice: Why, no, no more than reason.

Benedick: Why then your uncle and the Prince and Claudio Have been deceived. They swore you did.

Beatrice: Do not you love me?

Benedick: Troth, no, no more than reason.

Beatrice: Why then my cousin, Margaret, and Ursula Are much deceiv'd, for they did swear you did.

Benedick: 'Tis no such matter. Then you do not love me?

Beatrice: No, truly, but in friendly recompense.

Then Claudio and Hero show both of them two pieces of paper written on by Beatrice and Benedick, which reveal their love for each other.

Benedick: Peace, I will stop your mouth.

Kissing her.

Write your own love story . . .

Questions to think about before you write

■ Are your lovers forbidden to be together like so many of Shakespeare's characters?

■ Is one or both of them in disguise because they are running away from something else?

■ Perhaps their love is doomed from the beginning? Or could they live happily ever after . . .

TOP TIP

Use this area to plan your characters before you write. What are their names, where are they from? What do they look like, and what are their personalities like? Do they have friends who have influence on them?

Turn the page for more room to write

Test your Shakespeare knowledge
with this tricky crossword

Across

1. Oberon's mischievous fairy servant. (4)
3. A famous type of Shakespearean poem which has 14 lines. (6)
6. Romeo is from the Montague family, Juliet is a . . . (7)
7. Titania, Queen of the Fairies, falls in love with . . . (6)
10. Complete this play title: Much Ado About _____. (7)

Down

2. Egypt's glamourous queen. (9)
4. A symbol of love which rhymes with part. (5)
5. Where Shakespeare's company of actors mainly performed their plays. (5, 7)
8. A lovesick character who pins poems around the forest. (7)
9. Finish this line of poetry - Rough winds do shake the darling buds of . . . (3)

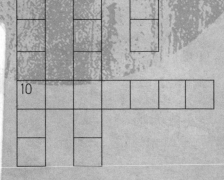

Disguise, I see thou art a wickedness

(Twelfth Night)

Put a man in a woman's costume, and you have a normal actor playing a female role in Shakespeare's time. Then, while that actor is playing a woman, get him to dress in disguise as a man. So you have a man dressed as a woman dressed as a man! Add to that girls, played by men, falling in love with the men who are dressed as girls dressed as men . . . do you give up?

This chapter is all about characters concealing their identity. Some of them simply wear a mask whereas others choose to dress up as someone from the opposite sex. More unfortunate characters such as Bottom in *A Midsummer Night's Dream* have a spell put upon them.

Enjoy reading these pages and creating your own funny stories of disguise, but keep your wits about you. Things are not always what they seem.

Top disguise accessories

Hat

Moustache

Old woman's clothes

Sunglasses – or normal glasses
if you don't usually wear them

Wig

Mask – best used at a masked ball

Superhero outfit – best used
at a fancy-dress party

List your top 5 fancy-dress outfits

1. ....

2. ....

3. ....

4. ....

5. ....

What happens next?

Edited excerpt from *The Winter's Tale*, Act III, Scene 3

Bohemia. A desert country near the sea

Old Shepherd: What have we here? Mercy on 's, a barne? A very pretty barne! A boy, or a child, I wonder? . . : I'll take it up for pity, yet I'll tarry till my son come; he hallow'd but even now. Whoa-ho-hoa!

Enter Clown (the old Shepherd's clownish son)

Old Shepherd: Here's a sight for thee; look thee, a bearing-cloth for a squire's child! Look thee here, take up, take up, boy; open't. So, let's see—it was told me I should be rich by the fairies. This is some changeling; open't; what's within, boy?

Clown: You're a made old man; if the sins of your youth are forgiven you, you're well to live. Gold, all gold!

Old Shepherd: This is fairy gold, boy, and 'twill prove so. Up with't, keep it close. Home, home, the next way. We are lucky, boy, and to be so still requires nothing but secrecy. Let my sheep go. Come, good boy, the next way home.

TOP TIP

Try reading the passage aloud to help you understand what they are saying.

Some questions to think about before you write:

- Is the mystery baby a girl or boy?
- What do they call the baby?
- Do they keep the baby and gold secret?
- Do they raise the baby as their own, or do they try to return him or her home?

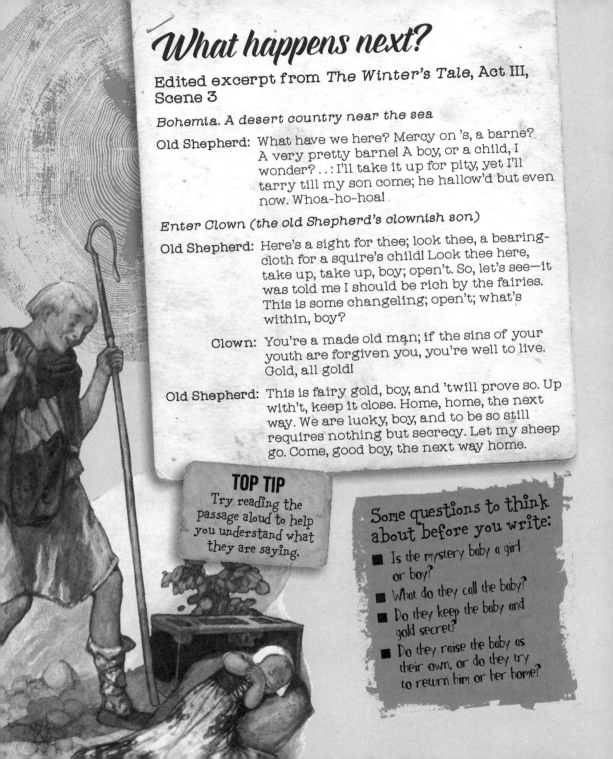

Edited excerpt from *A Midsummer Night's Dream*, Act V, Scene 1

Bottom: I must to the barber's, monsieur; for me thinks I am marvellous hairy about the face; and I am such a tender ass, if my hair do but tickle me, I must scratch.

Titania: Or say, sweet love, what thou desirest to eat.

Bottom: ... I could munch your good dry oats. Methinks I have a great desire to a bottle of hay: good hay, sweet hay, hath no fellow.

Titania: I have a venturous fairy that shall seek The squirrel's hoard, and fetch thee new nuts.

Bottom: I had rather have a handful or two of dried peas.

Some questions to think about before you write:
- What kind of animal's head have you been given?
- What does that animal like to eat?
- What does it like to do?
- How does it speak?
- How do your friends react when they see you?

Write a diary entry about waking up and discovering that you have an animal's head.

Write a funny story about long-lost identical twins

Confusion takes place in *The Comedy of Errors*, Act I, Scene 2

Antipholus of Syracuse:
Where is the gold I gave in charge to thee?

Dromio of Ephesus:
To me, sir? Why, you gave no gold to me.

Character Descriptions:

Twin 1: _____

Best Friend: _____

Twin 2: _____

Best Friend: _____

Scene Description: _____

_____

_____

_____

_____

_____

_____

CONFUSED? YOU WILL BE!

In Shakespeare's *The Comedy of Errors* there's not one, but two sets of identical twins. And not only that, they have the same names. Antipholus of Syracuse has a twin brother named Antipholus of Ephesus. They were separated in a shipwreck 25 years ago. Both twins have servants called Dromio, who are also identical twins.

In your story give each twin a best friend, and then imagine the moment when each best friend bumps into the wrong twin.

Write a conversation

You may have heard these expressions before, but did you know that they were written by Shakespeare?

Write a piece of dialogue (also known as a conversation) between two characters using at least 5 of the expressions on the left.

TOP TEN SHAKESPEAREAN EXPRESSIONS

1. green-eyed monster
2. dead as a doornail
3. in a pickle
4. for goodness' sake
5. blinking idiot
6. as white as driven snow
7. laughing stock
8. what the dickens
9. laugh yourself into stitches
10. vanish into thin air

Who are your characters? Write their names and a brief description here:

Character 1: ....
....
....

Character 2: ....
....
....

You can draw a picture of them in these frames:

.... : _____
(Character 1)   _____

.... : _____
(Character 2)   _____

.... : _____
                                 _____

.... : _____
                                 _____

.... : _____
                                 _____

.... : _____
                                 _____

.... : _____
                                 _____

.... : _____
                                 _____

.... : _____
                                 _____

.... : _____
                                 _____

What happens next?

Sir John Falstaff is broke. He decides to woo Mistress Page and Mistress Ford, who are both married, so that he can swindle some money from them. Unfortunately for Falstaff they work out that he is not honest in his love for them and decide to play tricks on him. In this scene the ladies try to persuade Falstaff to hide in a laundry basket so that Mr Ford does not find him and go wild with jealousy.

Edited excerpt from *The Merry Wives of Windsor*, Act III, Scene 3

Mrs Page: Look, here is a basket; if he be of any reasonable stature, he may creep in here, and throw foul linen upon him . . .

Write what happens next, but from Falstaff's point of view. What is he thinking and how does he feel?

Here are some words which have been used to describe the character Falstaff:

boisterous

lively

cowardly

funny

mischievous

dirty-rotten scoundrel

outrageous

thief

liar

conman

fat

drunken

comic

rogue

Write a story about a fancy-dress party where you aren't recognised

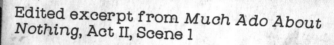

Edited excerpt from *Much Ado About Nothing*, Act II, Scene 1

Beatrice: ... will you not tell me who you are?

Benedick: Not now.

Beatrice then mentions the name 'Signior Benedick'.

Benedick: What's he?

Beatrice: I am sure you know him well enough.

Benedick: Not I, believe me.

Beatrice: Did he never make you laugh?

Benedick: I pray you, what is he?

Beatrice: Why, he is the Prince's jester, a very dull fool ...

A masked ball is a useful place for a writer to create some mystery or some comedy. At the masked ball in *Much Ado About Nothing* the men wear masks, but the ladies do not. So when Beatrice dances with Benedick, he knows exactly whom he is dancing with, but she is left in the dark. She chats away to her mystery dance partner, and talks about Benedick, calling him boring. So the audience is left wondering, does she know she's dancing with Benedick ... or not? What do you think?

You've probably been to lots of fancy-
dress parties. Have you ever been
to one where your friends didn't
recognise you behind your outfit?

Draw a secret disguise

Edited excerpt from *Twelfth Night*, Act I, Scene 2

Viola: *(talking to the Sea Captain)*
I prithee (and I'll pay thee bounteously)
Conceal me what I am, and be my aid
For such disguise as haply shall become
The form of my intent. I'll serve this duke . . .

Viola has been shipwrecked and separated from her twin brother, Sebastian. She believes he might be dead, so has to find a way to survive on her own. She decides to try and get a job in the household of Orsino, Duke of Illyria, but in order to do this, she must pretend to be a boy.

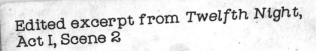

Viola, dressed as the boy, Cesario

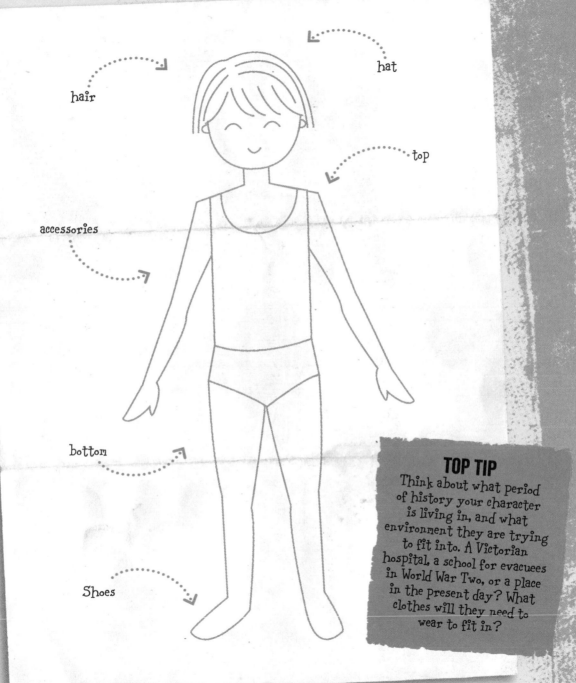

hat

hair

top

accessories

bottom

Shoes

71

TOP TIP
Think about what period of history your character is living in, and what environment they are trying to fit into. A Victorian hospital, a school for evacuees in World War Two, or a place in the present day? What clothes will they need to wear to fit in?

Write your own comedy story

There is so much fun to be had when you're in disguise. Using the character you created on the previous page, write a funny story of a case of mistaken identity.

TOP TIP

Think about who is telling the story. Is your character, who is in disguise, telling the story? Or is your story being told from the point of view of a character who is taken in by the disguise?

Turn the page for more room to write

Can you guess which of Shakespeare's play titles have been rearranged in these anagrams?

BATCH ME

☐☐☐☐☐☐☐

HEM PET TEST

☐☐☐ ☐☐☐☐☐☐☐

TALKIE IS YOU

☐☐ ☐☐☐ ☐☐☐☐ ☐☐☐☐

LOAVES BULLS ROOST

☐☐☐☐'☐ ☐☐☐☐☐☐'☐ ☐☐☐☐

SWEATER LET THIN

☐☐☐ ☐☐☐☐☐☐☐'☐ ☐☐☐☐

HALT ME

☐☐☐☐☐

WIERDNESS FOR IVY WORM

☐☐☐☐☐☐ ☐☐☐☐☐ ☐☐ ☐☐☐☐☐☐

NAILED TRUE MOJO

☐☐☐☐☐ ☐☐☐ ☐☐☐☐☐☐

Tell sad stories of the death of kings

(Richard II)

If you ever thought that members of a royal family were a well-behaved and moral bunch of people, you only need to have a quick glance at the plots in Shakespeare's plays to be proved wrong. The kings, queens, princes and princesses that Shakespeare writes about get up to all sorts of things, from murder to getting drunk in bars, to disguising themselves and escaping from their castles to marrying commoners, as well as, of course, leading their men into battle.

Many of the royal characters that Shakespeare wrote about were based on real people, including kings and queens that you might have heard of, such as King Henry VIII and Cleopatra, Queen of Egypt.

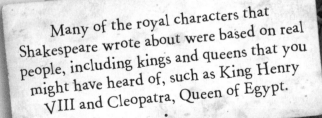

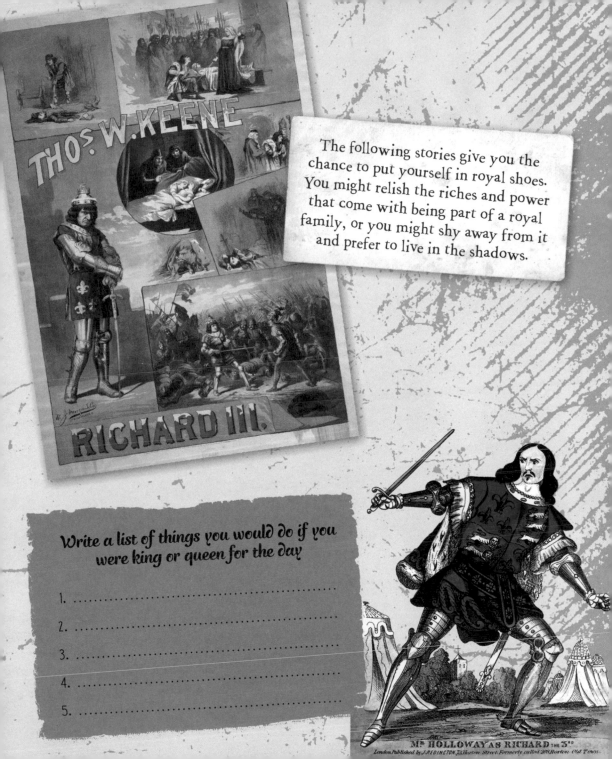

The following stories give you the chance to put yourself in royal shoes. You might relish the riches and power that come with being part of a royal family, or you might shy away from it and prefer to live in the shadows.

Write a list of things you would do if you were king or queen for the day

1. ....
2. ....
3. ....
4. ....
5. ....

THOS. W. KEENE

RICHARD III.

MR HOLLOWAY AS RICHARD THE 3RD
London Published by J. REDINGTON 73 Hoxton Street Formerly called 208 Hoxton Old Town.

Write a pep talk

Shakespeare writes a rousing speech for Henry V to deliver to his troops who are at war with the French. It's designed to make them more courageous and to rally them together.

Quotations from Henry's speech to his troops, *Henry V*, Act III, Scene 1

Then imitate the action of the tiger;
Stiffen the sinews, conjure up the blood . . .

Now set the teeth and stretch the nostril wide,
Hold hard the breath, and bend up every spirit
To his full height . . .

. . . And you, good yeoman,
Whose limbs were made in England, show us here
The mettle of your pasture . . .

I see you stand like greyhounds in the slips,
Straining upon the start. The game's afoot!

TOP TIP
Shakespeare uses animal imagery in his speech – try to do the same. Which animals will you choose to use?

Imagine that Shakespeare was going to write a speech for a sports coach to deliver to a team before a big match. Can you write a Shakespearean pep talk that will inspire your team to victory?

Plan the murder of a king

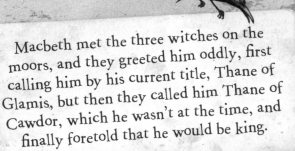

Macbeth met the three witches on the moors, and they greeted him oddly, first calling him by his current title, Thane of Glamis, but then they called him Thane of Cawdor, which he wasn't at the time, and finally foretold that he would be king.

Excerpt from *Macbeth*, Act I, Scene 3

First Witch: All hail, Macbeth! Hail to thee, Thane of Glamis!

Second Witch: All hail, Macbeth! Hail to thee, Thane of Cawdor!

Third Witch: All hail, Macbeth, that shalt be king hereafter!

Shortly after this Macbeth learnt that he had been given the title Thane of Cawdor. This set off a train of thought in Macbeth … to kill the current king, even though it would be morally wrong. His wife, Lady Macbeth, had no reservations about murdering the king, and she persuaded Macbeth to do the evil deed.

Fill in the speech bubbles in this scene where Macbeth and Lady Macbeth plan the murder of King Duncan while he spends the night at their castle.

Try using some of these words and phrases from the play, Macbeth, in your scene:

fatal

direst cruelty

courage

keen knife

bloody instructions

coward

who dares do more

be so much more the man

when Duncan is asleep

dagger

bloody business

wicked dreams

81

Write a story of escapism

There are two sides to Prince Hal, the son of Henry IV in Shakespeare's play *Henry IV, Part I*. One is the heir to the throne who knows he will be king one day and will have to face up to his responsibilities. The other is the young man who just wants to have fun. He disappoints his father by hanging out in bars with his friends, but by the end of the play his true, princely character is revealed.

This word cloud describes the two very different sides of Hal

low young dishonour
goodly greatness metal
sun princely riot beauty rude poor stain

Before you start, create your own word cloud to describe *your* characteristics.

Imagine that you are the heir to the throne, but you don't feel ready to take on the role. Write a story of a day or night when you escape from the castle and spend your time doing exactly what you want.

What's happening here?

Imagine you are Cleopatra's harp player. Write a diary entry about the day this picture was drawn. Describe what she might be saying in this scene and whom she might be talking to.

Quotation from Antony and Cleopatra, Act II, Scene 5

Cleopatra:
Give me some music; music, moody food
Of us that trade in love.

**Key characters from
Antony and Cleopatra:**

Cleopatra: Glamorous Queen of
Egypt, in love with Antony

Antony: Roman general and
joint ruler of the Roman empire,
married to Caesar's sister, but in
love with Cleopatra

Caesar: Joint ruler, with Antony
and Lepidus, of the Roman empire

Tragedies, histories and comedies

Shakespeare's plays can be split into three different types, tragedies, histories and comedies.

She's dead, deceased.
She's dead, alack the day!
(*Romeo and Juliet*)

A *tragedy* is a play in which something catastrophic occurs and will usually result in the death of a main character.

His guts are made of puddings
(*The Merry Wives of Windsor*)

A Shakespearean *comedy* will usually involve a case of mistaken identity, one or more sets of lovers, a complex plot and, of course lots of puns, funny insults and clever word play.

A kingdom for a stage, princes to act
And monarchs to behold the swelling scene
(*Henry V*)

A *history* play is based on real events and real people; however, as Shakespeare wrote primarily for the entertainment of his audience he would often be flexible with the truth.

TRAGEDY	HISTORY	COMEDY
Antony and Cleopatra	Henry IV Part 1	All's Well That Ends Well
Coriolanus	Henry IV Part 2	As You Like It
Hamlet	Henry V	The Comedy of Errors
Julius Caesar	Henry VI Part 1	Cymbeline
King Lear	Henry VI Part 2	Love's Labour's Lost
Macbeth	Henry VI Part 3	Measure for Measure
Othello	Henry VIII	The Merchant of Venice
Romeo and Juliet	King John	The Merry Wives of Windsor
Timon of Athens	Richard II	A Midsummer Night's Dream
Titus Andronicus	Richard III	Much Ado About Nothing
		Pericles, Prince of Tyre
		The Taming of the Shrew
		The Tempest
		Troilus and Cressida
		Twelfth Night
		The Two Gentlemen of Verona
		The Two Noble Kinsmen
		The Winter's Tale

How do you prepare to duel?

Edited quotations from *Richard II*,
Act I, Scenes 1-3

King Richard II: *(setting the challenge)*
Be ready, as your lives shall answer it,
At Coventry upon Saint Lambert's day.
There shall your swords and lances arbitrate
The swelling difference of your settled hate.

Both knights declare:
And as I truly fight, defend me heaven!

Lord Marshall:
Sound, trumpets, and set forward, combatants.

You are a knight and you are about to have a duel, possibly to the death, to defend your innocence and your honour. Write an account of what's going through your mind as you get ready to fight.

Imogen, Princess of Britain, leads a number of adventures in the play *Cymbeline*. Choose one of her adventures from the list below, and write your own story about what happens to her.

- Secretly marries her one true love, Posthumus, a commoner
- Disguises herself as a boy, and calls herself Fidele, in order to escape murder
- Travels to Wales, disguised as the boy, Fidele, and becomes a servant
- Accidently takes some poison, believing it to be medicine
- Works as a servant for a Roman general who is attacking Britain

Well then, here's the point:
You must forget to be a woman;

. . . O Imogen,
Safe mayst thou wander, safe return again!

His daughter, and heir of's kingdom . . .
. . . hath referr'd herself Unto a poor but worthy gentleman.

I am sick still, heart-sick . . . I'll now taste of thy drug.

Write your own royal story

Shakespeare was inspired to write plays about real royal families from the past. Choose a royal family from history to write about. It can be a story of love or war, or it could be a story of adventures and misdemeanours.

Decide on these details before you write:

- Country (e.g. England, France, Spain)
- Period of history (e.g. 1492–1501)
- Royal Family (e.g. The Windsors)
- Main character (e.g. Princess Grace of Monaco)

TOP TIP

Once you've chosen your main royal character to write about you can make up friends for them, just as Shakespeare did.

Glossary

arbitrate	settle the dispute
barne	child, baby
bearing-cloth	christening garment
bequeath	give up, hand over
bounteously	generously
changeling	child taken by fairies
combatants	fighters
Death brag thou wander'st in his shade	Death claims you for his own
deceived	given false information
eternal lines	eternal verse
fair	fair face, beauty
foe	enemy
foul	dirty
hallow'd	shouts, yells
Jester	a professional joker at medieval court

languish	waste time
lease	period of loan
mettle	spirit
mounted	lifted high
ounce	lynx
pard	panther
poor-John	dried fish
prodigious	not normal
recompense	repayment
referr'd	given
Saint Lambert's day	Feast Day of St Lambert, 17th September
sinews	nerves
speculation	power of knowing
temperate	calm
tender	young or sensitive
Thane	a man who had land, ranked with an earl's son
Thy bones are marrowless	your bones have no bone marrow in them, they're hollow
troth	true
untrimmed	lacking ornament
venturous	adventurous, daring

Answers

Page 35

```
O R E P S O R P C E V C V Y S
N U C W Z D H A Z U O O M D F
R O G T A P L P V Y W B R R R
U F R W Q I S D Z P Y A M I I
T W K E B S P R I T E R N D
Y E I A B L S G E S G B I M
Q K N T P O H Y R I A F E U P
B C G R C O B W Q R Q L S S
E D R O S H J O P L U L X S Q
B S N T X P H Q J U E X T W M
S A L O Y Z P T M F I J T G A
L P Q D H R U W M L X H Z W T
P O R C N H C N W O N A B H S
S M Q A U G K P Q S M C V I H
B U Z Z A F I M K P S B U K M
```

Page 55

1 ACROSS: PUCK
3 ACROSS: SONNET
6 ACROSS: CAPULET
7 ACROSS: BOTTOM
10 ACROSS: NOTHING

2 DOWN: CLEOPATRA
4 DOWN: HEAR
5 DOWN: ROBE DEER
8 DOWN: THEA(RE)
9 DOWN: MAY
(BRLADO / ND O) ORLANDO
HREARE

Page 44

Diplodocus (4)

Terrific (3)

Supercalifragilisticexpialidocious (14)

Page 75

BATCH ME
MACBETH

HEM PET TEST
THE TEMPEST

TALKIE IS YOU
AS YOU LIKE IT

LOAVES BULLS ROOST
LOVE'S LABOUR'S LOST

SWEATER LET THIN
THE WINTER'S TALE

HALT ME
HAMLET

WIERDNESS FOR IVY WORM
MERRY WIVES OF WINDSOR

NAILED TRUE MOJO
ROMEO AND JULIET